Quilts *from* Nature

Joan Colvin

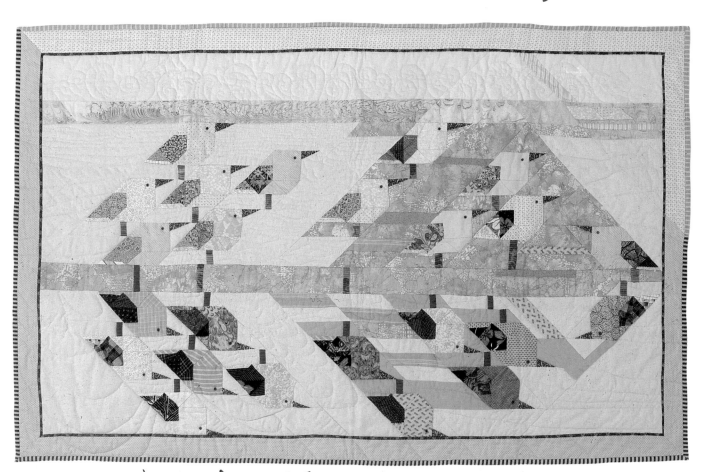

That Patchwork Place®

To Betty—
One of my dear QOE friends, who took in a stranger, and created the loving atmosphere where work can take place. I'll never forget, and I'll always be grateful.
love, Joan

Credits

Editor . . . . Barbara Weiland
Copy Editor . . . . Miriam Bulmer
Text and Cover Design . . . . Judy Petry
Typesetting . . . . Karin LaFramboise
Photography . . . . Brent Kane
Illustration and Graphics . . . . Karin LaFramboise
Stephanie Benson
André Samson
Joan Colvin

Quilts from Nature ©
© 1993 by Joan Colvin

That Patchwork Place, Inc.
PO Box 118, Bothell, WA 98041-0118 USA

Published in the United States of America
Printed in the British Crown Colony of Hong Kong
98 97 96 95 94 93   6 5 4 3 2 1

Acknowledgments

Special thanks to Bill, who has always supported my art projects in every major way; to my mother, Dorothy Chase McClane, who first showed me and continues to show me the joy of fabric; to my children, who were always cheerfully part of any discovery process; and to Judy and Frank, who know how to nurture the artistic process.

Thanks to my California quilting friends. I am especially grateful to Stefi Kuster, who shared her considerable expertise, and to Polly Allen and Kay Cashman of the Monday Morning Group. Thanks also to all the members of the Foothill Quilters, and to Susan Thompson, Nabuko Otsubo, and Joan Apel.

I appreciate the Washington friends who encouraged me: Priscilla Stuart and her friends in Anacortes; Mary Hales; Margaret Fouts; and especially Hazel Hynds, who included me in Quilters on the Edge. To this warm circle I owe much: Nell Moynihan, Gail Bohrer, Suzanne Hammond, Julie Mitchell, Betty Oves, and Kim Radder.

And thanks indeed to the entire staff of That Patchwork Place—a superb organization!

Library of Congress Cataloging-in-Publication Data
Colvin, Joan,
  Quilts from nature / Joan Colvin.
    p. cm.
    ISBN 1-56477-026-5
    1. Patchwork—Patterns. 2. Quilting—Patterns. 3. Nature (Aesthetics) I. Title.
TT835.C648 1993
746.9'7—dc20   92–41488
                                                     CIP

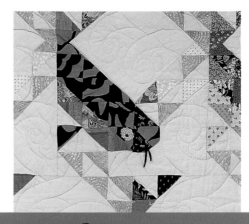

Contents

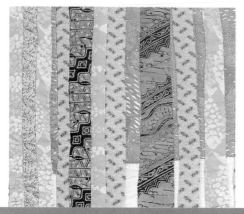

Introduction

SAYING WHAT YOU WANT TO SAY

The more you read and the longer you live, the clearer it is that everything's been said before and probably better.

What's equally clear is that things are forgotten, or haven't yet been heard by the young—or that it's nice to hear some things again. Since repetition is soothing sometimes, I will tell you about my quiltmaking even though it may be much like yours.

After forays into other media, I returned to quiltmaking as if to a warm and welcoming friend. Whether you sew alone or within a circle, you cannot escape a feeling of kinship and understanding: work produced by others strengthens you; it is given freely, offering no threat and intending none. Not many human endeavors permit such sharing.

I love quiltmaking because you can make a thousand fresh starts, try a thousand new directions, and feel you have a thousand friends—sometimes without ever leaving home!

In this book, it is my intent to try to tell you what I do as a quiltmaker, in the hope that it will encourage you to trust in and follow up on your own ideas. If you are new to quilt design, I hope you will enjoy using the patterns for my quilt designs. Using a pattern is a lot like reading a good book: You like what the author has said; rapport is established; you say to yourself, "I could have written that," or, "I wish I had been able to say that," or, "I believe that, too." In return, quilt designers are deeply gratified to find their patterns used by others.

Like literature, quiltmaking is an art form that evolves from life experiences. It offers a resting space. You can have periodic spurts of productivity without committing to the life of an artist. The fabric lies comfortably in quietude, waiting for your free moments to play and experiment. It doesn't dry up, congeal, or decay. Organization and cleanup require only one sack for pieces, one shelf for stashing stuff, and one minute to do it.

I hope this book will encourage artists accustomed

to other media to try fabric. It is an enriching and challenging experience to watch creative expression make a transition from one art form to another.

Most of all, I want to encourage any and all to work fearlessly with fabric to interpret original designs. When you have the desire to say something, I want you to feel you can work it through for yourself. You can create a piece of art from your own designs, arising from your own perceptions. Somewhere on a continuum, starting with a simple Four Patch block and extending to wildly complex assemblies, you can find the way to say what you want—and it will feel good.

WHAT'S TO KNOW? WHAT'S TO TEACH?

You'll need a few solid skills so your work won't sag, disintegrate, bleed, or otherwise embarrass you. I've included several basic techniques in a short chapter at the end of this book, but assume that you have acquired some skills already—or will consult other books for additional help. Many excellent books cover these quiltmaking basics, including the books in The Joy of Quilting Series, published by That Patchwork Place.

I must admit that I am not a good source for technical guidance. I tend to take risks with seductive fabrics and end up more often than not with a wall quilt that sheds, molts, and requires periodic trimming! But some order is needed. It is no fun to find that you have assembled something upside down after long hours of work. It helps if the way you lift your pieces to assemble them, the way you pin, and the way you turn or otherwise position pieces has become an automatic routine. Develop your own shortcuts, memory joggers, and safety rules—working basics that will allow your hands to operate smoothly and effectively while your brain roams a bit over the design, assessing the work in progress. That way, the assembly process is restful and satisfying. Ultimately, this is how good ideas come to mind.

If you do assemble something backwards, don't toss it. Consider revising your design concept. Could the pieces be a reflection? An echo of the major pattern on the back or in the border? I am a firm believer in the "happy

Joan Colvin

accident," a major factor in any honest artist's success. For years, quilters have made substitutions for fabric they have prematurely used up, and they have also inadvertently and then purposely turned and twisted designs. Their work is the richer for it. Identify how you feel about the "mistake," and if undoing it is the only answer, do it with good grace and learn from what you did. Check your procedures to prevent similar recurrences. (That would really make you mad!)

HOW CAN YOU MAKE A QUILT THAT'S UNIQUE?

Quiltmaking, like other art forms, can be defined in terms of periods, cycles, or fashions, with changes in style and content. Think of the rich history of quilting. Some think we are living during quilting's finest hour, but look back at our traditional beauties—the Baltimore Albums, Double Wedding Rings, and Log Cabins—all of them historical statements and art from the heart.

In quiltmaking as in art, one begins at a specific point in time and then experiences various styles and approaches during a lifetime. (You are in your Picasso period? I'm in my Andrew Wyeth!) It may be overwhelming to set yourself the task of making a major statement or doing something totally unique. What may seem to you on the "cutting edge" may well have been done by your great-great-grandmother and laid away as a mistaken effort! So it's not likely to be the art style you choose that will make your work unique, nor will it be the subject matter, nor even the technique. It is the life and energy you bring to your current interest that will make your work unique. It is the passion, or the mood that you convey. I will never fear to be a little old lady doing pansies. There are pansies and there are **pansies**!

What is more important, I think, is to help you find a way to inject some life and humor into your idea. Maybe profound beauty isn't always attainable, but a quick moment of delight or the recognition of a small truth causing an intake of breath—that's what it's all about.

I cannot think of a better place to find life and humor than in the graceful workings of nature. Most of the quilts in this book started with nature watching.

DESIGN COMES FROM WHAT YOU PERCEIVE

We learn from observation, and what a lot there is to learn! Color is often not what you think it is. Sand, after all, is gloriously multicolored when you see its grains up close. Lines are veins, connections, outlines, etchings of nature. And as for texture, think of bark, rocks, leaves, feathers, and fur. Your subconscious must absorb and translate it all.

I'm nearsighted, so I get an initial "whole" impression when looking at things far away. I see a person's stride and bearing, energy and demeanor from afar; later I work out who it is. That approach is helpful in design: One sees the flock as a unit or as a pattern without the distraction of details (what they are doing or who they are, for example).

Because I don't get all the information initially, when I'm ready, I look intently and see great detail. The point I'm making here is that there are so many aspects of looking and seeing. Sharpening your observation skills improves your design abilities. Essentially, the more you see, the more you have to say. (And it is easy to edit out too much information.)

Much of design is the perception of relationships. If you can become aware of sizes and shapes and what they do in combinations, you can control the effect. I won't attempt to deal with this aspect of design in any professional way here, but I will give you a few suggestions— steps I've devised to guide myself through the design process. (See "Designing Quilts," page 22.) Remember, though, that people who **do** art often **do not read** about it. The joy of primitive work is the enthusiasm in playing with detail . . . sometimes a lot of it, sometimes almost none. The power in more tutored, more sophisticated art often rests on the fact that much of the primitive still shines through.

So follow your own interests and instincts to the extent that you are amused and intrigued, and never let the lack of formal training hold you back!

How to Use this Book

If you want a quilt pattern—no fuss, no muss—turn to the quilt designs, which begin on page 34. I have included complete directions for creating your versions of several of my designs. Other patterns will require some independent choices on your part; with these quilts, I have given you block cutting and piecing directions in the hope that you will make up the blocks and design your own settings and backgrounds.

If you want to try to create your own "quilts from nature" and want an idea of my thought processes as I work, read the description of how the Trumpeter Swan quilt evolved, beginning on page 9.

Artists new to fabric may be interested in the progression of steps and the reasoning behind certain design decisions as they relate to fabric blocks, but can and certainly will diverge from my personal choices at many points.

On the other hand, I hope that those of you new to designing will take courage from the sort of meandering I do, and realize that having an artistic bent is not a mysterious ability; it is only permitting yourself the luxury of taking time to play with color and shape—a lot like the "messing around" we allow and expect of children. If you like that sort of thing, and can be gentle with yourself when evaluating your early attempts, you'll be drawn into the creative process with ease. Please don't let any inner critic discourage you. Immerse yourself in shape and color, and go in any direction that looks interesting. In art, nobody can be really sure of anything, so the field is wide open and waiting for you!

Joan Colvin
Bow, Washington
November 1992

DEVELOPING THE IDEA

I see trumpeter swans—sweet old things in the muddy fields of Skagit County. They are rare, so we mustn't disturb them in their privacy as they grub away to get fatter for an uncertain future.

How to keep my vision of them? They are in a clumplike flock (quilt subject matter from the earliest times—a repetitive pattern). White on the dark earth. There must be water; swans always have a reflection. Well, it could be *dark* water, and marshy, weedy looking. The real swans are too busy to care that their legs are showing awkwardly, gooselike. So forget that image. Go for the reflection, have them swimming.

White on dark this time. I've never done that. Do all the swans have to be white? Probably, for a sense of unity. (See "Unity," page 23.) Immature swans could be there, allowing for color and feather variations, but they would have to be secondary to the white swans. Some warm neutral colors would be fun, too, making the white starker. I am seeing this:

A Design from Nature

What distinguishes a swan from other birds— besides fluffy bodies and long necks that can go any direction? What makes trumpeters unlike other swans? I see this form in my mind:

Time to find a picture. My bird guide shows *Olor buccinator* the largest swan, and he *is* different from other swans.

"Narrow flesh-colored stripe at base of mandible is hard to see but diagnostic."

Well, I'll decide about beaks later. Anyway, the neck is long and narrow, as I'd pictured, so I make a rough drawing.

How can I best create these birds in fabric? Absolute realism is possible. I'm thinking of the intricate, graceful portrayal of herons as done in Asian stitchery. Or the entwining, patterned work of the English designer William Morris, in the 1890s. Both of these realistic portrayals would involve a lot of appliqué. Do I want to appliqué this time? I'm already intrigued by the idea of a flock, and flock means repetition, and repetition is classic Early American piecing. I'd rather do that.

Assuming I can put together a swan block, let's just see if I even *like* the idea so far.

There are plenty of other positions for the swan. Why am I sticking with this one? It's here. It's easy. It's working so far. Get out the graph paper.

Fit a mature and an immature feeding swan together. The sketch above suggests a diamond block. A square on end would be a lot easier, because I can use right-angle triangles and squares. A little shading will show light swans on dark ground, so I begin to see what will happen.

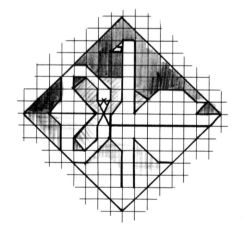

Assessing the design so far, I consider several criteria.

Size: How big should the basic triangle and square unit be—1", 1½", 2"? Much larger? Much smaller? Does that change my concept?

How large will the block become? How large will the quilt become? Sixteen units of 2" make each block 32" across; therefore three blocks would make a 96"-wide quilt, which is pretty wide. If I use 1½" units, the quilt will be 72" wide, a much more manageable size. Do I want a square quilt, though?

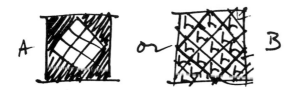

If I decide to do version B, what happens to those partial blocks?

Effect: I am reminded less of a flock now than of a little set of scenes, each swan pair in its own frame, like a Currier and Ives Christmas design.

Design: Are the lines and shapes pleasing? I'm not satisfied yet. I went awfully fast from picture to graph paper, not really trying out other placements for the swans in relation to each other, or in terms of the effect of the reflections. I am *very* unsure of the shapes formed when the blocks are juxtaposed. These shapes are awkward now, and I doubt that color will correct it. (See "Negative Space," page 25.)

I'll try something else. What if I go back to a square block and put the swans together as closely as possible? I'll shorten the swan neck by one unit to condense the block.

darks here could form bad negative space

various colors joining here might prove unpredictable —

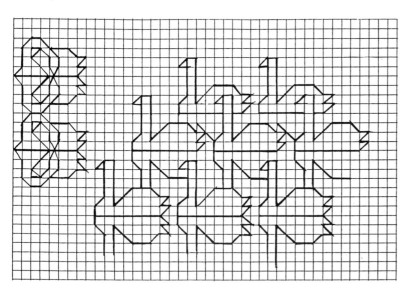

That's more like the effect I wanted. Let's try integrating the two swans another way, in a rectangular format, changing the body shape slightly and enlarging the block as before because the neck really does have to look longer.

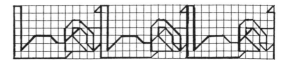

That looks better. Now about the second row of blocks. How far down? How far over? I play with the block placement, looking for the most satisfying connections. My aim is to find a secondary pattern or flow in the background behind my major design (the swans). Using a copy of my sketch on graph paper, I cut the first row apart from the second and move it back and forth. Clearly, the simplest setup is to line up the blocks row to row.

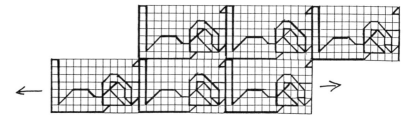

However, this placement lines the necks up into vertical sashing and they disappear, so that's not good at all. Try the next-easiest placement, offsetting the blocks by half, row to row.

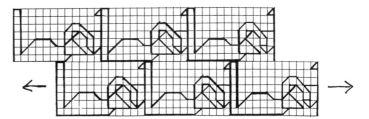

That's not too bad. It would work, but I have lost the area for the major swan's reflection. So, I try offsetting by only a quarter block, instead.

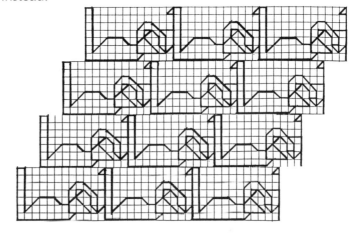

Now, see what is happening? There are better connections. Instead of the powerful swan necks lining up every other row, it takes four rows to line them up, and your eyes follow down diagonal lines to the left. At the same time, the curved swan neck pushes your eyes back to the straight neck so you can start the diagonal slide down again. Controlling eye movement may sound silly, but if you think of your tongue rolling around to savor a taste, it makes sense that your eyes do that too! (See "Visual Movement," page 24).

Let me assure you that you don't have to identify or put into words what you see and feel when assessing a design. Things happen; the design works. It works all right; it works superbly. You'll know it's right and you don't really need to know why.

At any point in design, one can change and take a new direction. Do not close any mental doors. It is possible to be satisfied at many different levels. The more you play with a design, the better your chances for something unusually good; no guarantees . . . sometimes your initial impulse is just fine.

So right now, I like my swan design. Next, I need a few measurements. At this point, my block is twelve units wide and seven units high. If I can get it eight units high, it might be better proportioned; the mathematics will be easier. Let's try.

added row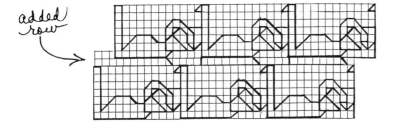

When I slip a row in between, the swans look rotund, I think, especially if the reflection idea is fully implemented. I won't do it.

FINALIZING SIZE

Now it is time to consider size again. How many make a good flock? What will be the viewing distance? (See "Viewing Distance," page 25.) What size units can I comfortably handle? How large does that make the finished piece?

My mental picture had about eleven major swans, no more than three abreast, but this certainly isn't a sacred number. As to size of unit, I am comfortable with a 2" unit. A 2" triangle can still be split in half for details and is large enough to make a statement from a mid- to far vantage point. I would be willing to try 1½" units; I could use up lots of scraps that didn't make the 2" cut!

Using 1½" units, the block would be 18" x 10½".

Using 2" units, the block would be 24" x 14".

A queen-size quilt must be 60" x 80", without the border. Are the dimensions in that range? Let's do a few calculations.

3 x 18" = 54"	3 x 24" = 72"	
7 x 10½" = 73½"	7 x 14" = 98"	or 6 x 14" = 84"
21 swans	21 swans	or 18 swans

If I don't mind a few more swans, I am in a good range with either unit. I can make a wall hanging if I decide on minimal borders, or I can stretch to a queen-size quilt.

Now it is time to make up a sample of each size to compare, and to see what they actually look like from various distances. I take a shortcut here. I cut two pieces of white fabric, each 2" x 14"—one for the neck and one for the bottom part of the swan's body. I place these strips on a dark background. A roundish blob of white fabric above the white strip at the bottom fills in the swan feathers enough to give the effect of the overall size, especially if I step back and squint a little.

I'll do the same thing for the smaller unit, with strips 1½" x 10½".

After evaluating both swan "mockups," I choose the smaller unit, thinking the swan is still big enough to dominate, but the smaller triangles will give me flexibility without having to split them in half. Too, I can reduce the flock size somewhat by incorporating some plain blocks. Besides, I've never worked with 1½" units before. I'd like to keep the total size of the quilt down, for ease in handling.

CUTTING TEMPLATES

Deciding what units in what shapes will be needed to compose the whole block involves a few personal decisions. I like both large and small spaces in my designs. (See "Spatial Relationships," page 24.) I also like to leave large spaces for flowing quilting patterns to hold the layers together when the quilt top is completed. In addition, it's too much work to break up one piece of fabric unless you especially need a faceted look (or happen to have little pieces already cut!).

So, here are the larger shapes that I expect will be one color.

After looking at the design again, I prefer not to commit to a single color anywhere else. (See "Room to Play," page 26.) That means the small units can be:

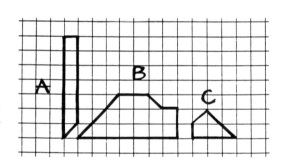

(For making and using templates or, alternatively, using rotary-cutting techniques, see page 99.)

SELECTING FABRICS

Now I am ready to pick up some real fabric pieces, cut them into the 1½" units I've chosen, and set up a real block. Sometimes, I just plunge in and let the fabric guide me by trial and error. This time, however, I bring that original vision to mind—white swans on dark earth. That's the mood I want to convey. Such a high-contrast effect is easy to create but I am left wondering where the middle values might be effective. (See "Contrast," page 24.) A little preplanning on paper will save time and fabric. I shade in dark where I'm sure, leave light where I'm sure, and then crosshatch what is left as the middle value.

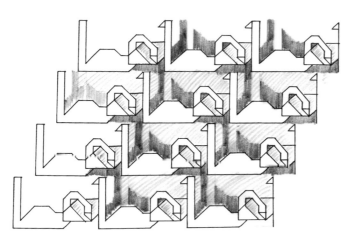

Now I can see the desired secondary pattern in the dark values emerging. It makes a sort of circle around the swan back and its reflection and becomes a chain link throughout the quilt. I'll keep that in mind, though I don't want it to be overwhelmingly noticeable. What's left for middle values are the second swan and the reflections. That's simple enough.

I start by sorting out darks and lights, trying not to read "black" for *dark*. I squint my eyes and then grab colors that seem intense, concentrated, and heavy. That pile may include dark green, dark gray, navy, brown, black, and maroon—all of which, when viewed in a lump, will look blackish. Cold colors can be used with warm. (If you question the juxtaposition of colors that don't seem to be in the same color families, walk outside and really see what nature does.) Since I expect this quilt will be viewed at mid- to far range, I now step back that distance to stare at my pile of dark fabrics, again squinting a little to heighten my perception by dulling the details; up close, you can be fooled by pattern. I set aside any that don't seem dark enough (to use for medium dark).

Stack the whites too. I stay with two or three whites, because I am depending on that color to balance the choppiness I plan for the reflections. (Actually, many different whites will look the same from a few feet away.)

From this point forward, there are many options, none more right than another. This is how I proceed with the swans.

I take time to sort through my scrap bag for likely pieces, pressing and cutting them into the various shapes I might be using. I make a great many more triangles than anything else.

Next, I cut swan necks and swan bodies, using Templates A and B. I find that I can use up little pieces of white I have on hand by breaking up the swan's tailfeather area; in addition, assembly will be easier if the swan template isn't too irregular.

Last, I cut a number of darks, using some of Templates F and G, and a lot of D and E, all in dark colors, because I plan to integrate many darks and I won't have very many solid, one-color areas.

LAYING OUT A FEW BLOCKS

Now, my aim is to get a few blocks laid out in front of me but not necessarily assembled. I find it easiest to work on pieces of fleece, and I keep on hand about a dozen that are roughly 18" x 24" (larger than most unassembled blocks). I can position all the small units on the fleece until I get the block laid out, and I can move the pieces of fleece around on the floor to see how the blocks will fit together. When I have to clean up the room quickly, I place a piece of newspaper between each block laid out on the fleece; that way, I can stack the unassembled blocks easily without fear of losing any of the little pieces or having them move out of position. That's just one way, and it works for me.

Using five or six pieces of fleece, I lay in the knowns—swan #1's neck and body. Then, I do some darks, to begin to see the range of color, or contrast. I choose some light neutrals for swan #2: some slightly tan, some slightly rose, getting a little variation in color but staying very light. After all, these immature swans aren't really colored, and I'm exaggerating but not straying from nature's hues.

In selecting fabric for swan #2, I have started colors for each of the blocks. Using some of these same tones, I begin to fill in the reflection under swan #2, then move left under swan #1 with medium fabrics, in large and small scale. Think of water sparkling—refractions, ripples—but remember it is muddy water, so don't overdo it. I work down from the swans to the dark water I've already started to lay in, using more darks and dark mediums as I near the bottom. I try not to distort too much the "chain link" pattern made by the darks, but I'm not going to be so fussy that I can't integrate the light water with the dark.

That leaves the trickiest part: relating the colors where four blocks come together. Should I have spent more time planning what happens there? Part of the unifying process in design is controlling the flow of color, which in turn controls the eye. That is why I want to avoid having four different colors of water come together where four blocks meet. I do not want a random meeting. (I could have chosen to break the blocks in a different place, where random colors wouldn't be a problem. Many traditional quilt patterns *depend* on this randomness for richness and variety.)

I realize that I didn't think this part through, and now I want to get a diagonal flow of color, like water eddying. There is nothing I can do until I see a number of blocks together, so I make at least eight blocks, choosing colors for everything except those tricky corners. Then I arrange the blocks so that they begin to look good together, and when I'm sure of the placement of this group of eight, I assign them numbers (pinning a number to the fleece) and sketch a little "master plan."

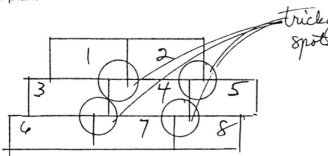

Now, I can plan the eddies, filling in all the corners. There is a lot of room to play with color in the reflections and the water, and I begin to wonder about other things. Is there a warm glow, maybe from the sky, that would light some swans and water more than others? Should the outer swans be darker, or shadowed? Should some birds fade out entirely? What seems right? Shouldn't some reflections be crisp and sparkly, others almost nonexistent? I put myself there in the marsh. What am I seeing and enjoying?

This process may go on awhile, and my color choices might require subtlety, bravery, certainly a lot of mind changing. Some blocks go together quickly; others are left until the end because they don't work yet. As a few become acceptable, I begin to assemble them in the evenings, saving my "prime time" energy in the morning for more color choices.

FINALIZING THE DESIGN DETAILS

Before I begin to piece the first block, I need to settle the question of swan beaks. In the back of my mind I am thinking I will appliqué some good beaks, later. I don't want to deal with this detail now, so I piece in a head-colored beak, in case the one I appliqué doesn't require the whole triangle space.

PIECING THE SWANS

As I mentioned earlier, it is important to use the piecing method that works for you. Sometimes I like to hand piece in the company of friends or family. When I'm impatient, I speed piece by machine. What works best for me is to do the more intricate parts by hand and the larger pieces by machine. I'm still carrying around my numbered fleece rectangles, so it's no problem if little fabric pieces lie on the fleece only partially assembled.

After piecing some of the blocks and sewing them together, I realize that I must deal with the outer edges of the quilt top, where there are partial blocks left that I haven't yet designed since I wasn't sure what would look best in those areas. Now, when I play with some rough sketches, I at least have some sense of the "largeness" of my project, and I can assess my enthusiasm as well. How do I like my work so far? If I do like it, am I interested enough to carry it forward to a large finished work? If not, how can it be modified before I put *all* the blocks together?

I am happy with the swans so far, but they are looking awfully *big* and awfully *white*. I have to stand farther and farther back. I decide to add more dark around the edges so that the flock doesn't take up the whole space. Two rough possibilities cross my mind, both acceptable.

I choose A because it is a little more like the traditional, repetitive pattern typical of classic pieced quilts, and that was my original vision. It would also be a good configuration for a bed quilt. I like B a lot; it would be nice for a wall hanging, and I'm tempted to try it, too. I like the large white shapes going off the edge balanced by the large dark space; a different swan design, maybe a single, would be interesting there.

If I'm doing A, partial blocks will taper off from the main design; now and then, only one of the swans will be needed and fewer reflections will result. It appears that, horizontally, I should have the equivalent of three-and-a-half blocks across, before adding the border. In other quilts I've designed with blocks offset by half, it was easy to design a half block to fit the half spaces. Here, because I have a quarter-block offset, I will really have to do each irregular space individually. Since I'm thinking "darks," that won't be too difficult—simply a matter of counting out how many units wide each partial block should be. I make another sketch to scale, and this time I number the partial blocks in my diagram so I can set them up on fleece rectangles and number them just as I numbered the blocks.

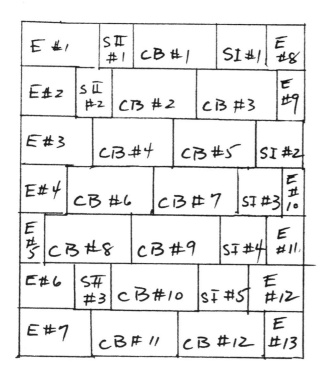

Width:

Complete Block (12 units)
Swan I (7 units)
Swan II (5 units)
Edge (what's left*)
* figure each one separately.

VIEWING THE PIECED QUILT TOP

Now, it is time to stand back and look at the completed top. For me, there is a toddler's body-shaking urgency to get the layers together and to see what the actual quilting will look like. But, "Be still, my heart," as someone so aptly said. This is the time to stop and really look at the design effect.

Hang the work where you can glimpse it from different angles, and trust what you see out of the corner of your eye. Realize how important this stage is. You hope you will get little jumps of excitement, and your expectations for successful completion are high. But it is rare to be perfectly, perfectly satisfied at this stage. If you're like me, there may still be some conflict—some nagging little detail. Keep walking around the work, taking sidelong glimpses.

It is a good idea to wait several days before you proceed. If there are changes that really should be made, take the time to make them now for peace of mind later. Evaluate the effort required for changes versus the value you place on this work. (Sometimes, you've already "cooled" on a piece, and you are willing to simply take what you've just learned on to another quilt.)

In the case of the swans, a change was needed—not a monumental change, but an important one to me. I felt that the head on swan #1 looked too gooselike and that the essence of the trumpeter was a slim, straight, level head. Why didn't I see that earlier? Surely, I'd been working with the block long enough. My answer may perhaps help you to understand what the design process involves.

I had been placing the total swan body in its surroundings, in relation to the secondary swan, and seeing large contrasts in color and value. My focus had been very broad for a long, long time. I moved from the smaller unit to the whole and back, from general to particular and back again, from light to dark. This zoom-lens, in-and-out motion is what allowed the design to emerge in scale, viewable from more than one distance, its components orderly and related. I tried to keep all options open as long as possible. When I did identify my dissatisfaction with the head, I could recognize that I had known it all along, but had considered it a refining detail, which it was.

To correct the swan head, I must say I tried many things before the moment of inspiration came. My first attempts to appliqué a realistic beak over the existing triangle were very unsatisfactory; the beak looked trivial. Up close, the sculptured appliquéd piece looked nice, but from a distance, the wavy dark shape interrupted the white swan head, and an ugly little negative space developed.

None of my beak designs worked. Standing way back, I realized it might be the shape of the head that needed changing. By extending the beak, I could get the lovely slim head that differentiated the trumpeter from other birds. Yes!

Final Beak:

Next time, I'll extend the beak, but will have to adjust angle of background water .. and probably make swan taller + longer. See, one thing leads to another!

To change an already assembled block, the quilters I admire get out their seam rippers. I appliqué instead. I know my tolerance level for technical perfection is terribly flexible and my ability to wait almost nil. Know yourself, and do what you must to make the necessary changes.

PLANNING THE QUILTING LINES

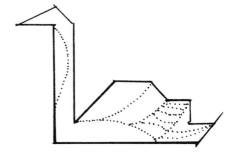

After the quilt top is completed to my satisfaction, it's time to plan the quilting-stitch pattern that will join the top to batting and backing. I decide to rely on the quilting stitches to define the feathers in the swans.

If I could think of a good reason why all the feather lines should be identical, I would do them that way. But that would mean drawing them on ahead of time—and I'd rather "wing it." I can't resist seeing if something slightly different might work out better. Each one draws itself. If too much variation occurs, I will go back and change some in order to unify the design.

CHOOSING A BORDER

I have a sense that the border for this quilt must be dark, continuing to reduce the perception of the size of the swans. I will use a narrow bright border first to define the outer edge of the quilt top, then a wider dark border. The binding will be wider than the bright line, but subtle, not eye-catching.

SUMMARY

Think of all the junctures where other design decisions would have led me in different directions. See why some painters have spent their lives exploring a single subject? A life devoted to swan designs seems a bit incomplete, but I may certainly try other configurations. I would like to do a long swan quilt, in pastels, perhaps, with flowers, in light water. And I could go back to the half-light, half-dark wall hanging. We'll see.

Now, when you look at the color photo of my finished quilt (page 59), you may realize that you do not see at *all* what I have just described as my design process. You, as the viewer, don't really need to know what I was thinking. But what kept me interested while I was working is exactly what gives vitality to my finished piece.

Does that help to explain? I want this design analysis to be the incentive you need as a living, lively person to put some living, lively ideas out where they can be enjoyed first by you, and then by the viewer. Complexity is not required. But satisfaction is. It is fun to be around someone who is happily and creatively occupied. For me, there is almost no greater joy!

Designing Quilts

LEARNING FROM NATURE

As a quilt designer, my challenge is to observe what is there, be aware of how it actually *appears* (or better yet, how it could appear if life were perfect), and then translate this mental picture into a design form that preserves the essential elements but is vastly simplified. This requires some judgment, to determine what can be condensed graphically—simplified, straightened, emphasized, or de-emphasized. If I go too far, I might as well become a Cubist and quit worrying so much about detail. If I don't go far enough, I dare nothing at best or become too cute at worst. This is my own game, you understand. You'll want to pick your own. In general, though, design is a process of choosing— what can be kept and used, what should melt away.

Sometimes we can express the orderliness of the universe in geometrically clean shapes. But then again nature's lines dangle and angle in unusual directions, escaping capture in simple, geometric boxes. A neat block of wood startles you with a knot.

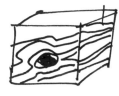

Quiltmakers know that when you feel controlled and neat, you tend to choose orderly arrangements, with stacked blocks and precisely cheerful fabric.

Nature can be like that, too. Look at honeycombs and crystals, ladybugs and cumulus clouds, sunflowers and pineapples. But nature also has its wilder side: wood grain and sand patterns in tidal flats, angular lightning and craggy rocks, tree branches and crocodiles. Our grandmothers would have said, "There is a fine line between order and chaos." That's a bit heavy; after all, we are just trying to decide how to use line and pattern, and we might choose chaos with no ill effects whatsoever. But my perception of chaos is that it isn't very much fun to watch. I don't know about you, but I design and make quilts for pleasure.

I get real pleasure from Asian brush paintings because they capture so simply and swiftly the essence of things. Of course, it sometimes takes a lifetime of practice to be able to do such a painting in a few brushstrokes, and the artist *knows* the subject by then. You can respond to what you know. The sooner you make an attempt at design, the sooner you will understand the dynamics and feel comfortable with your attempts and interpretations.

Speaking through fabric isn't any different than speaking through other art forms. You can approach it from one of two directions. One is to just wallow in fabric, using it to form lines, texture, depth, and pleasing harmonies, letting it lead you to a design statement. The finished design may or may not be a recognizable subject. This approach is perfectly legitimate and is especially appealing to abstract thinkers.

It also avoids the dangers of the second approach, which is to become overly caught up in authenticity. If you choose to come from this second direction, assess the subject till you have a feel for its nature, vigor, and surroundings. Decide what's attractive and what's not, what's distinctive. See if it looks natural in geometric forms, or can be made to appear more natural with the addition of quilting lines to help soften the overall effect. Perhaps it should be appliquéd. Can it be exaggerated in some way to be different or amusing? At the conclusion of this design process, you may be more than ready to find fabric to express what you've discovered.

USING THE ELEMENTS OF DESIGN

As I move from a rough initial concept toward a more definite finished design, I consider certain elements of design to help me assess my work as I proceed. A basic understanding of them and how they are interrelated will help you as you explore the design process. For any given project, some of the elements will be very critical and some will have almost no significance at all, but it helps to mentally check them off as you finalize your design. Sometimes I deliberately choose to ignore one or more. There are all sorts of considerations in the formation of good design; what follows is a discussion of those I have found pertinent and useful when designing quilts. For a more in-depth discussion of design, ask for books at your local library.

Unity

Think of the whole quilt at once, so you don't get preoccupied with a little pattern that doesn't belong anywhere. You want the design to work as a whole. Repetition of a color or pattern is an easy way to do that, or a gradation of value from light to dark, or a directional design that points or chases itself. Traditional pieced patterns are already expressions of unity; scenic designs or those that focus on a single object are more susceptible to clutter or disarray.

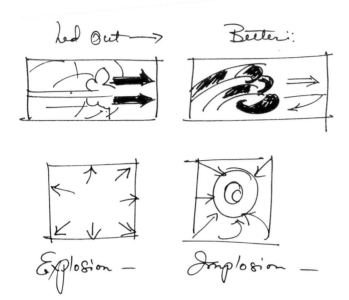

Led Out →   Better:

Explosion —   Implosion —

Visual Movement

Where does the eye go? What do you see first? Usually the eye is guided from light to light; it can jump spaces successfully. For variety, light can be broken up, but if the placement of light areas is too choppy, you will lose the desired effect. The viewer's eyes will tire from whirling around a quilt top with no place to rest.

Be careful not to let the design elements lead your eye right out of the picture. Avoid design shapes that point and lead you to the outer edge before you have time to appreciate the heart of the work. Watch for these effects as you design and it will become an intuitive process.

Contrast

As long as we are considering the placement and movement of light within a design, think of how important stage lighting is for spotlighting, highlighting, setting a mood, or giving direction. The placement of light helps create contrast. The painter Rembrandt produced powerful results with just a touch of light on a mostly dark ground. Assess your design idea in terms of contrast: Would a high contrast between light and dark (as in the Trumpeter Swans quilt, page 59) be best, or does your idea call for a smooth flow with little or no break, little or no emphasis beyond the gentle transition of colors?

Spatial Relationships

When everything in a design is the same size, boredom is a possibility. But you can look at this another way: blandness can be very calming. Variation in size breaks things up, for good or for bad. Consider the illustrations below. You can create lots of different designs simply by varying the size of the S.

The S is only one shape, and you can get a lot of variety from just the S alone. As you add more shapes, which may also be varied in size, you begin to have quite a powerful array of components; some repetition in size may be desirable for a calming effect.

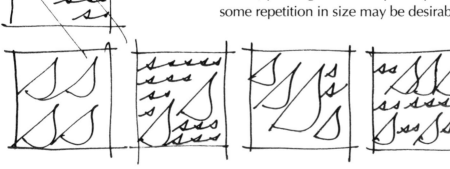

At some point, then, it is important to stop and assess the effect of variety in size in your work. For example, you may begin with a small block of triangles and then discover that it needs a complementary, larger triangle for variety and visual interest.

Simplified diagrams help you see what will happen in the whole quilt top. You don't have to draw accurate representations on graph paper; try picking an easy shape or an alphabet letter to quickly see where you might end up and to help you think of the whole rather than the part.

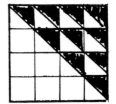

Other reasons you might need variety in size would be to show off fabric to its best advantage or to leave room for a particular quilting design.

Negative Space

Looking for negative space can be an eye-opening concept, especially if it has never been pointed out to you in the past. In the illustration at left, look for two images—a facial profile and the negative space behind it. Try to see each as a separate, distinct shape. Once you've noticed the reverse of the profile, it is difficult to see again the pleasant face. That ragged edge just intrudes—more so if it is a darker color. This happens routinely in design; when you get preoccupied with an object, it is easy to forget to check out the shapes surrounding it.

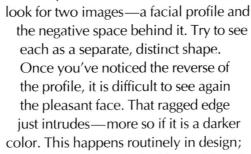

From frustrating experience, I can warn you to experiment ahead of time with how your blocks will come together, so that no unpleasantly shaped or colored negative spaces develop. In fact, with careful planning, exciting secondary patterns often emerge at the four corners where blocks touch each other. Avoiding difficulty at these places forces me to examine and improve them—a wonderful design opportunity not to be missed.

Viewing Distance

Most artists would like viewers to enjoy their work from any vantage point, so it is important that you shift your focus as you work. It is very easy to get absorbed in the design and color-selection process at a working distance (arm's length) and miss what happens when you stand back from your work. For example, the brushstrokes on the backdrop for a stage set look entirely different when viewed up close rather than from the rear of the theater!

Make sure you view your quilt top from a distance throughout the working process. Shapes and values are perceived differently, depending on where you are standing. Squinting used to be one's best

*Carousel Friendship Quilt
(page 77) in process.*

bet. Now you can buy a reducing glass, or use instant photography. Zooming in and out is critical to assessing good design.

As you assemble blocks and then join them, seam allowances disappear and size relationships change a little. Sometimes a design looks a little crowded or awkward where large-scale patterns come together. Luckily, more often it works the other way, and you are delighted by the happy accidents—unplanned side effects!

Room to Play

I like to leave some aspect of my plan unsettled, leaving room to see what happens. This can be a subtlety in block placement, but more likely it is an area where color variation can occur as the mood strikes, or it is a background area as yet unformed in my mind. Learn to balance the risk of wasted time versus the joy of spontaneity. If I know everything about the quilt top before I start cutting and stitching, I am always less excited and motivated to finish it. On the other hand, if I didn't plan carefully enough and it isn't going well, it is hard to stay interested.

What works best for me is to plan fairly well; plunge in and get started; go back and refine; plunge in again with more knowledge and enough momentum to almost finish; assess the results and correct a bit; then finish the top and quilt at my leisure. I also find that if I save some intriguing little detail for the very end, after quilting, I'll finish, and more than that, my creative interest stays alive until the end. Do be careful with "whimsical" details, however; they have been known to overpower or severely detract from otherwise good work. For example, in my current work, I am trying to pull back from excessive ornamentation. I don't mean to ruin the fun, but it is important to be selective when it comes to finishing details.

Designing for Ease of Assembly

The assembly process is a personal matter. Some of the most gorgeous quilts are technical wonders, and some are not. I can love and appreciate the exuberance and adventure of a collagelike expression in which nothing matches or touches and all the strings hang out. But I can be deeply moved by the architectural perfection of the work of Jan Myers-Newbury, for example, as well as by the work of immediate friends whose needles are miracles of accuracy and for whom each stitch is a challenge. Their standards for technique are enormously high.

How you will assemble a design is a major decision, involving how you feel about technique, your personal vision of the end product, and your own patience and commitment. (That does not mean you always have to do the same thing!) Read enough about quiltmaking techniques to find a comfortable approach. What follows is the process that works best for me.

I choose easy-to-assemble shapes. I like little triangles and squares because you can use them like large brushstrokes to create movement, and it is easy to sew them together. I like diagonals because they line up, whether large or small. If I'm improvising, I don't care what the angle is, but if I'm lining things up, a 45° angle will take me anywhere I want to go with the design. Diagonals are dynamic lines that lead the eye through a composition.

I usually use one of two distinctly different assembly processes. One is like making the muslin for an original dress pattern—working loosely, pinning, tacking, basting, changing, and molding. In other words, nothing is secure.

The other process is more like what you do when you've bought a dress pattern—cutting, stitching, pressing, and trimming in the prescribed sequence. I swing back and forth between these two, depending on how much I know about where I'm heading. I've already confessed to employing any expedient solution that occurs to me. I neaten things up at the end the best I can, without redoing anything major, and I quilt over lumpy seam intersections shamelessly. Then I move on. That's it. I've had my fun.

Quilting to Add Dimension

Anyone new to quiltmaking may need a little extra perspective here. Up to now, we've talked about the design of the quilt top, assuming you will sew together little pieces of fabric to complete it.

Some people are less interested in the piecing process than in the quilting to follow. They prefer a single unadorned expanse of fabric and decorate it with stitching lines, making intricate line patterns with some slight dimension. The result of expending years of labor and pounds of thread can be a simply exquisite, textured line drawing on a plain canvas. These beautiful, whole-cloth quilts are highly prized.

Planning the quilting for a pieced quilt, however, requires additional thought. You must consider the design lines in the pattern of the fabric as well as the lines that develop as the individual units are cut out and sewn together. The delicate little quilting stitches add a third line dimension. The interplay of these three elements is critical to the success of your work.

In the early days, quilting stitches were utilitarian—to hold the stuffing in place. Otherwise, the pure cotton would bunch up and slip around during washing. The tinier and the closer together the quilting stitches were, the sturdier the quilt. (I can imagine that doing this got old in a hurry, and the quilting lines began to wiggle and curl off in unimaginably complex and highly diverting ways.) Today we can use fiberfill battings for the stuffing. They are manufactured so that the fibers stay in place and require less closely spaced quilting stitches. That means we can do what we wish with the quilting stitches.

Common approaches to quilting involve outlining or setting off a colored area. Deciding how close to the object this outline stitching will be is partly an artistic decision and partly a technical one. (How many layers of fabric can you penetrate with your needle and still keep the stitches even?)

Another approach is to quilt inside a shape.

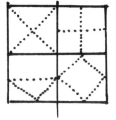

Or, you can quilt right over a piece in a more random pattern.

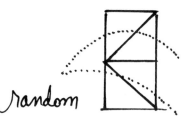

You can connect the corners, the sides, or both.

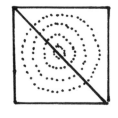

You can superimpose any design wherever you wish.

You must also consider how to mark the quilting lines on your quilt top so you can see where to sew, yet easily remove the marks when the work is finished. For more information on marking methods and quilting in general, I recommend *Loving Stitches* by Jeana Kimball.

I eliminate the marking process whenever I can because I love to improvise as I go, varying the design just as nature's design lines vary. By the third or fourth block, I know in general which lines are working best, and I can revise earlier ones if need be.

A useful technique to employ when you are undecided about where quilting lines should go is to loop thread around anchor pins that follow the line you think you want to follow with your stitches.

Quilting almost always looks beautiful if the stitches are of a uniform length and evenly spaced. However, you can't depend on the quilting to rescue a badly designed or a badly pieced quilt top (Sometimes, in a very densely or elaborately colored design, the quilting stitches get lost and are hardly worth the effort.) You must also decide how puffy, how much dimension and texture you want in the finished product. Ask to see the effect of the different battings available. Observation and experience will help you determine what's most satisfying to you. I have used a variety of battings. I've concluded that I really can't guess at the effect. I must make a little swatch, using the backing fabric I've chosen, since I cannot bring myself to unsandwich and unquilt.

As you design a block, don't forget to plan ahead for this final stitching process. You may wish to leave large blank spaces for flowing quilting that connects to the pieced blocks. Minimal quilting is acceptable, too, if the intricacy of the design is sufficient.

In the quilt designs included in this book, I have indicated where I used quilting lines to enhance the overall appearance. Generally, I try to soften the look of angular pieces with rounded quilting lines that cross over most areas enough to hold the quilt sandwich together.

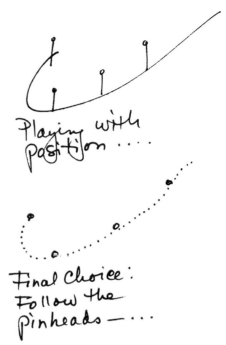

Playing with position . . . .

Final choice:
Follow the
pinheads — . . .

CHOOSING COLOR AND FABRIC

Nature's Guide to Color

We are stopped in our tracks by rainbows and northern lights, by the intensity of the turquoise waters off Barbados, the brilliant Indian red of the Arizona canyons. Irish green is not misnamed. No wonder we work to preserve the clarity and freshness of an earth that produces such color.

Though it is sometimes difficult to think beyond the striking colors of the rainbow, the blue sky, and green fields, there is much more. Brilliant clear color in nature is not a rarity, but remember that color at midday differs from color at dawn or dusk. The quality of light in the south is warmer in tone than the quality of light in the north. Think of how the light changes in a summer thunderstorm or during a winter snowfall. What was brilliant and clear becomes

muted and grayed, opening up an entirely new set of color experiences. Cloud banks, plumage for protective coloration, drying grasses—these are also exquisite displays of nature's colors.

As quiltmakers, color in almost unimaginable variety is available to us in fabric. The vast array makes a most attractive "palette," which is why, I think, a painter could be lured to fabric art.

I hesitate to suggest a general approach to color. Personal taste changes and evolves over time, and your color sense does too. As quickly as I can verbalize a rule about color, I can find a wonderful way to break it successfully. Now I seem to favor grayed neutrals, but any color of any intensity can be used to good end, no matter the current color trends. It is important to work with colors that are pleasing to your eye, but also to step a bit beyond your color comfort zone. If you look intently at the intricacies of *nature's* color selections, you will find ways to enrich yourself as well as your work.

Fabric Selection

They say fabric is seductive. Through the ages, people have been inspired, comforted, frustrated, and charmed by the magic of fiber. We are lured by color, texture, and line in all the combinations that surface design permits on fabric.

If you are enchanted by a particular fabric, you are then faced with a challenge: What will it do? What could I do with it? For some fabrics the answer is quite clear, but with others the answer is not always immediate. Those fabrics often end up on the shelf while your subconscious works to find a way to use them to their best advantage.

Some fabrics can be cut into tiny colored units and used to achieve an effect similar to the way Georges Seurat painted thousands of individual specks of color on a canvas to create a painting. Other fabrics are best used in larger pieces because of their spectacular beauty of design. I often think I will choose one wonderful fabric and squeeze everything I can from it, in combination with one solid.

Where do we start in making a fabric selection? Rembrandt, for instance, allowed himself just four colors and look what he mixed up! We have to make choices, but we don't always have to limit ourselves in the same way, or to the same degree.

If I'm thinking of a scene, I might limit my palette to establish a mood, using the qualities of light, from warm to cool, and light to dark. If I'm making a piece for a room with an established color scheme, I'm more likely to think bold or subtle, large or small scale, clear or grayed tones, contemporary or classic, and from these initial thoughts, a plan for the desired color range emerges.

If you wish to learn to use fabric and color in a new, less controlled way, try the following color exercise. One day, use a piece of everything in your scrap bag, no matter how unappealing it might seem initially. Toss fabric pieces, letting them fall where they will, and then fill in your random composition with neutrals. This exercise will broaden your sensitivity, as you see how unexpected combinations read from a distance. Use speedy cutting-and-stitching techniques to assemble strips or blocks made up of these multicolored, random combinations. "Random" is the key word for this exercise.

For a less random procedure, though it may not sound so, try my method of working with fabric and color. First, I make a broad, preliminary selection of fifty or sixty fabrics; then I add small pieces from my scrap bag. Stacking and spreading a palette of fabric around me on the floor (still in large and small portions), I sometimes group lights and darks, but I'm not really particular about order. I just want to be able to see a wide range of fabrics, either directly or in my peripheral vision.

I begin to build up color, laying little pieces of fabric on a piece of fleece in the general shape of my design. (See "Laying Out a Few Blocks," page 16.) I cut a little hunk from whatever fabric catches my eye and put it in place as fast as I can, not worrying about shape except in a very general way. If my color ideas are emerging, I whack out the fabric quickly, wasting some. Ideas can be fleeting, and I'm anxious not to lose the impulse I'm following. While I have the momentum and flow so important to getting the right effect, I pile the fabric wherever it's needed—I'll think about shape, fabric grain, and templates later. (I call that part the housekeeping mode of quilt design.) Laying in color goes on until I'm tired, interrupted, or I come to what feels like a natural stopping place. Later, I can assess what I've done and make corrections and adjustments. I ask myself:

➤ Are the values right?

➤ Is there too much contrast or not enough?

➤ Are the color and design transitions too abrupt or too wishy-washy?

➤ Is the overall color plan any good?

➤ Does the overall design concept work? If the plan was for gentle and neutral, is it pleasantly subtle? Too subtle? Too boring?

➤ If the plan was for dynamic pattern and color, is it bold and thrilling? Or is it too splashy or even tacky?

➤ Are the shapes going to be the right size for the fabric I've chosen? Should the design be modified?

➤ Is there anything else it needs? Is there any expectation or excitement on my part? Can I pinpoint why or why not?

When I'm past these questions and am generally on the right path, I refine shapes: rearranging squares, triangles, and hunks; replacing several small pieces with one large; replacing a small scale pattern with a larger one. At the same time, I refine color choices, exchanging a cream for a pale peach or substituting a plain green for a patterned one, for example.

When you are using fabric as a paintbrush, it is difficult to separate a discussion of color from a discussion of shape. How you hold your brush determines the shape of the stroke and the intensity and size of the spot of color. How you position triangles and squares determines the same things. So throughout my work, my pieces are changeable at will. If I can't find a fabric that does the job, I piece my own and cut it up. These are my brushstrokes.

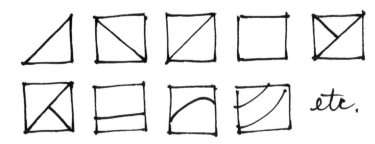

Sometimes, a special fabric does not show to advantage when cut into small pieces, so I decide to modify the design, changing several small pieces into one larger unit related to the smaller ones to better display the fabric design and color.

Finally, I get out templates, trim the roughly cut fabric pieces to the correct size, and attempt to sort out and put away unused fabrics. This may sound like a haphazard process, but for me, it's fun!

In the previous discussion, I have not separated color from pattern, because to me the *combination* is the key. It's what I see, and what my choice is at that moment. To add a further richness to the experience, you can consider texture. It is hard to resist the soft, finely woven cottons that are the staple of the quilt shop, but now and then, you need some "seasoning"—a rougher or smoother effect. Don't discount anything. I personally save up bits of silk—some antique pieces, some from ribbons or old scarves—to add texture to my quilt compositions. Finely woven wools in rich colors and old batiks are wonderful, too. Upholstery fabrics provide variety. Of course, how you plan to use your finished quilt should also figure in your fabric choices, so consider durability and washability. Back fragile fabrics with fusible interfacing for stability.

In the quilt directions that follow, I give you specific cutting directions for one block, but what I really want you to do is to get out a big pile of fabric, cut a lot of little shapes, and spread them around you as you build your own color interpretation of my blocks. Naturally, you can also examine the quilt photos for inspiration and guidance. Look closely at illustrations in books and magazines for the color effects you are seeking. Better yet, look outside. A flower that appears round and white from your porch might really be tan, yellow, pale peach, and cream, with striped petals and chewed-up edges. Work in the garden for a while and you are bound to come in with a fresh approach to color interpretation!

So, now it's your turn to make a quilt from nature, using the quilt patterns that follow as the springboard for your creativity.

Tree Birds

Tree Birds, by Joan Colvin, 1988, Bow, Washington, 78¹/₂" x 98¹/₂". A scrap quilt designed in traditional style, this stunning piece includes some antique and tea-dyed fabrics. Appliquéd beaks and eyes add to the colorful, exuberant effect.

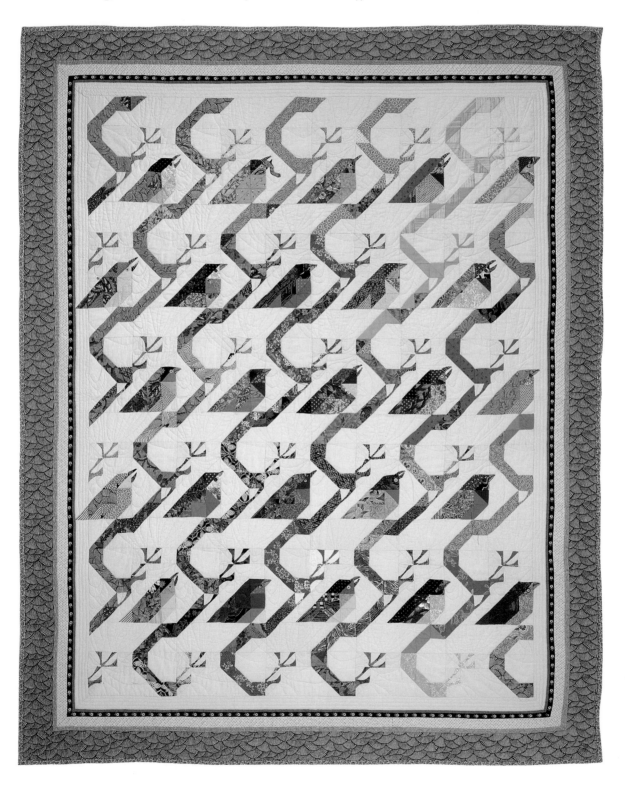